Glorious

Reflections of

Strength

To:
Bridgette

Thanks for a wonderful
and true friendship. May
God continue to bless you
and keep you near. The
support and help on this
project was most appreciative.

Love always

4/17/95

Glorious

Reflections of

Strength

Faye Swilley Manigault

Merging Worlds Publishers, Inc.
Atlanta, Georgia

Request for information should be addressed to:
Merging Worlds Publishers, Inc.
P.O. Box 2137
Smyrna, Georgia 30081-0998

Library of Congress Cataloging-in-Publication Data
Manigault, Faye
      Glorious reflections of strength / Faye Swilley Manigault

ISBN 0-9655253-4-1

Cover Graphics: Rob Jerome Jones, Atlanta, Georgia
Cover Design: Graphics Gallery, Atlanta, Georgia
Author Photo: Grady Meadows, III, Atlanta Georgia

Printed in the United States of America

Contents

This book is dedicate to the memory of my mother, Elaine Merritt Swilley, whose unconditional love and guidance made me a stronger person. And to my closet companion, communicator, supporter and nurturer of my dreams, John Manigault. Thanks John for your sensitivity, caring and understanding that you have devoted to this project. There is no one to whom I am profoundly indebted to than my loving husband. Thanks for always being there.

Acknowledgments

First of all, I would like to thank God for giving me the internal strength and the faith to write.

With love, thanks is extended to my husband and son for your support, unconditional love and allowing me the time to complete this project. To my father, Al Swilley and extended family, thanks for loving me through good and bad times. To my sister, Sherylle, your love, friendship and support I trust and admire. Thanks for loving me sis!

To my brother, Al, thank you for your enthusiasm, encouragement and positive input about this book; thanks for being such a joy! To my mother-in-law, Mother Lois, your support, prayers and selflessness fills my life with joy and happiness. To all my aunts and uncles, Mae, Harold Johnson and Denise Swilley, thanks for your love, loyalty and expertise.

A very special thanks to all my in-laws for your spiritual guidance and support. Thanks to my nieces and nephews for sharing your feelings and comments. To my cousins and

Carlora, thanks for your love and support of this project.

To my precious friends who encouraged me to be myself and move forward; thanks Jancis Newsome, Sharon Parks, Lois Smalls, Karen Fields and Tom McBeth.

I would like to express deep appreciation to Mae Johnson for your story and the initial editing of my work. It was also very important to have fellow writers that believed in my work. And thus, I would like to thank Ms. Carlora Turnquest for your special foreword message and editing assistance.

Thank you my niece, Tamisha Parker, for your child care assistance and patience. A special thanks to Ms. Claudette Strickland for your enthusiasm, suggestions, support, late hours and names for this book, they were most valuable. I am especially grateful to my pastors and church family of Ben Hill United Methodist Church. Thank you for your inspiration, prayers and spiritual growth.

Additionally, I wish to acknowledge the countless individuals who so generously offered ideas, and information. To all others thank you for being whom and what you are.

Finally, thanks to Deena M. Jones for believing I had a special story to tell, and for your help in bringing this book into final form.

Foreword

Six years ago, I had a very traumatic experience. My mother died after a long battle with breast cancer. How devastating it was for me to be without someone who had loved and taken good care of me all of my life. For a long time, I felt numb, depressed and in despair. During that time, I turned to many different avenues for strength and guidance. Out of all the avenues I tried, reading spiritual books was the most beneficial for me. They helped me find the strength I so desperately needed.

The book you are about to read would have been a great resource for me during my troubled time, and after reading it a second time, I realize that *Glorious Reflections of Strength* is a powerful book needed at all times in life, whether good or bad.

The author has creatively incorporated real life personal experiences from a variety of individuals with very different walks in life. The stories are sincere, positive, and most of all inspiring. While reading the stories, I could easily relate to many of the situations. Each story led me to the realization that all humans, no matter how different, are the same and share a connection beyond the physical realm.

What is most enlightening about this book is that it offers guidance on how to develop the strength many aspire for. These motivational tools work for anyone who is willing, faithful, and diligent in obtaining successful daily living. Thus, this book must be read and the principles practiced not once, but each and every day.

Through the short stories, poems, and quotes, you can discover how to overcome hardship, improve yourself, and begin or continue the search for whom you really are, and embrace your purpose on this earth. Also, you can learn how to better communicate with loved ones at home and individuals at work. Most of all, you will see that no matter what achievements you have made in life, and regardless of all the material possessions you may have, balance and success during change and adversity are not truly possible without acknowledging God and the great love that He has for you.

I am thankful that this captivating new writer has surfaced and that she is sharing her life principles with others. It is my desire that through these readings you will achieve the blessings and happiness that this wonderful new author continues to have.

GOD IS GOOD!

Peace and Blessings,
Carlora Turnquest, Screenwriter

Introduction

When I look in the mirror, it reflects a confident and motivated person that provides nurturing and care for others. I like what I see, especially since I've over come many adversities and obstacles in my life. I believe that the tools and skills shared in this book will encourage and inspire you twenty-four hours a day, seven days a week.

I started writing this book in 1997. It was inspired by a dream. In this dream, I was talking to a friend that was reflecting to me through a mirror. She told me to share my life experiences and the experiences of others. "This will uplift and encourage others to do better. Do not ever give up, follow your dreams and nothing shall stand in the way," she said ending the conversation.

I awoke feeling motivated and began to write my story. I realized that we all are reflections of each other. Just as my friend reflected what I should do, others reflect what you should do. We all have the ability to encourage and guide each other. This is why I included in this book the stories of others and what keeps them motivated. Perhaps their stories can help you.

As I began to write, I reflected to my mother and the many words of advice she shared with me. In particular, "Love yourself first, then you can love others without a challenge. Do not be afraid to take chances or risks; your short-term sacrifices are your long-term results. At the end you can see how close you've come to accomplishing what you wanted with the results you were expecting." Her words at the moment of beginning this project were very important to me. As I reflect back, I realize that I have not always been motivated nor have I always had good self-esteem. It is something I had to desire and allow God to move me into.

Staying focused and motivated is very crucial to me. By cultivating goal setting, finding my own internal motivation and developing my relationship with God, I have developed self-worth and self-esteem. This is very important especially being a mother and wife while working a job that requires a twenty-four-hour commitment.

I am sure this motivating book will enchant everyone who reads it. All of the contributors tell their stories on what keeps them motivated twenty-four hours a day and seven days a week. They further share how they balance their careers, have quality time with their families and personal time. The stories share their own challenges and triumphs that are uplifting and inspiring. This book includes high-spirited, motivating poems, intriguing quotes and daily reflections that will keep you enthusiastic each day.

The main purpose of this book is to help you stay or become motivated throughout your life experiences. It is my goal to make it simple, clear and helpful. This book focuses on practical matters through the use of true stories. Many people are faced with career and life changes that can appear overwhelming. This book helps during these transitional moments.

Successful motivators can be people from any walk of life, background and profession. These individuals have learned the keys to staying positive, despite what is going on around them. It is my desire that you utilize their stories to motivate yourself to be the best and do the best at all times. While this book of motivational stories can be a powerful tool, its success in your life depends on your involvement and attitude. You are the most important element in developing the inner strength required to create a successful life. Please enjoy!

EVERY LIFE
HAS A PURPOSE

Today I release and allow God to awaken me to my divine purpose!

EVERY LIFE HAS A PURPOSE

DAILY REFLECTION

Without doubt, every life has a divine purpose. Recognizing that you were created to fulfill an aspect of God's overall plan can be quite powerful. If you find yourself in the midst of dissatisfaction, unsureness and not being able to reach goals, perhaps you are off purpose. Meditate on the following words:

Shew me thy ways, O Lord; teach me thy paths.
Lead me in thy truth, and teach me: for thou art the God of my salvation; On thee do I wait all the day.

Psalm 25:4-5
King James Version

A day is an opportunity for you to endure. May the days ahead bring all the best, and may God richly bless you.

A Life Changing Transformation

Sharma Lewis
Student Minister, Children's Ministry

Sunday, February 13, 1994, I recall waking up to a bright, cool day, realizing that something was different. There was an unusual spiritual presence, an energy with me in my room. For some reason I felt extremely excited about going to church. I didn't know why, but I felt almost an urgency to go; the feeling was overwhelming. Little did I know that this day would change the course of my entire life.

I dressed as fast as I could and drove to the church. When I arrived at church, I sat in anticipation. My soul was stirring as the preacher spoke and the choir sang. I was sitting in my usual spot with my girlfriend when in the middle of the service, she leaned over and sarcastically said, "Why can't you sit still?" I looked at her and oddly enough, I couldn't comprehend why I couldn't sit still either.

As that service ended, I decided to stay for the next service

3

to support my friend who was preaching for the first time. My friend confidently stood up, walked to the podium and announced his scripture text and sermon title. Interestingly, his title was *"Have You Been Called?"* When he said the title, goose bumps covered my arms and before he was finished with the sermon, tears were uncontrollably flowing down my face.

Upon the altar call, I stood up and walked toward the altar. I knelt down at the altar and felt a warm presence surrounding me. I felt as if I was caught up in a time warp. There was a feeling of peace hovering over and around me. The feeling was so intense. I'm sure I hadn't ever experienced anything similar to it in my life. Suddenly, I heard a quiet voice speak to my soul, "It's time to stop running, preach my words." Immediately, I felt warm human hands touch my shoulders and utter, "It's time." The floodgate of my eyes opened and tears continued to flow down my face. My heart was racing. There was an intense feeling of excitement in the air. God had just spoken to me! And, I had just been called!

This all occurred at a time of great need. Before this moment, I had desires to go to medical school. Even as a young child my mind was set that I would one day become a doctor. But after applying to two medical schools, and both times being placed on the waiting list, I felt discouraged.

Why had I not been accepted into medical school? The question haunted me. My aunt suggested that I seek what God had planned for me. She said that being a doctor was my idea, but perhaps God had another purpose for my life. After hearing her words, I began to pray and ask "what is my purpose?"

On February 13, 1994, I accepted my call to the ministry and enrolled at Gammon Seminary at the Interdenominational Theological Center in Atlanta, Georgia. It took a tremendous amount of strength to release my job as a chemist and become a full-time student. I now realize that sometimes we are off our "Divine" path and it may require a lot of courage and strength to move onto it.

It is important for us all to realize that we each have a "calling," yours might not be the same as mine but just as important. If you are not on your Divine Purpose, then there can be much struggle and pain. You might find yourself experiencing tremendous ups and downs, good times and bad times. However, as you open-up and ask God's assistance, it will be revealed why, and what you are here for.

It takes courage and strength to then move on to purpose. But one thing you can rest assured of, upon your choice to be on purpose, the way and courage to step into it will be instilled within you. You will also be sent people to help you make this life changing move. It is truly God's desire for you to follow your "Divine Life Purpose."

In 1995, I was hired as the Student Minister of Children's Ministry. My job is to develop a comprehensive program for children to meet their spiritual, social, and educational needs. Now, here it is four years later and I am as motivated as the day I was called.

Knowing that I am on my correct path is one thing that keeps me motivated. Also, I am motivated by my service to God, which encompasses not only family, community and church, but all aspects of my life. I am always reminded of the scripture where Jesus tells his disciples that "He came to serve not to be served." (Luke 22:27 New Revised Standard Version). God has allowed me to see a glimpse of the ministry He has carved out for me. I know that there is so much more that I have not yet seen. My life is awesome, the struggle is gone and so are the disappointments.

Now, I am a physician, but a physician of another kind. I help people heal their lives by recognizing the God within. While I am now on my chosen path, it is my desire that all people be on their chosen path also. Perhaps my life changing story can serve as a reminder that you to have a "calling" all your own!

TODAY I WILL WORK TOWARD MY PURPOSE

Bridgette Sears
Police Officer

I must seek peace, surrender worldly desires, and create a vision of truth to obtain health, happiness, and prosperity. I must stop living my life by man's beliefs and concepts. I was made a unique person, by a unique Being. That means there is only one of me, and I was created for a specific purpose. I may not know what my purpose is right now but as I surrender my worldly desires, the closer I become to fulfilling God's purpose for me in this life. The more I do His will, the more I realize how important my role in this life becomes. The gift of giving and loving is so powerful that it disturbs all doubt and fear that the enemy hopes to prevail in me.

I now, realize that there is reality in a situation and there is truth in a situation. My carnal eyes see the reality that the crisis may bring, and my spiritual eyes see the truth in the crisis, which is there is no mountain too heavy for God to remove. I create a vision of peace throughout my situation and call forth the steps that God has ordered for me in this situation. I will sit still until His will is clear because the battle is not mine it's the Lords. Thanks, God. And so it is!

TO WORK

IS

TO SERVE

Achievement without service will not endure!

TO WORK IS TO SERVE

DAILY REFLECTION

Service is the key to success. If you find yourself struggling financially or having dissatisfaction in your job then perhaps you are not utilizing the service principle. The service principle is very simple, as you give, you shall receive. Therefore, as you give service you shall receive blessings and gifts blessed and multiplied. Ask yourself what service can I offer and meditate on the following words:

> Meditate upon these things; give
> thyself wholly to them; that they
> profiting may appear to all.

> 1 Timothy 4:15
> King James Version

When emergencies exist, people call for help.
Emotions run high and there is only a split second to make a decision.
Our true desire is to help save lives and prevent additional problems.
So, call the big red truck and we will be there to assist you.

True Humanitarians

Phillip E. Smith
Firefighter

*A*merican Heritage Dictionary defines a Humanitarian as "one devoted to the promotion of human welfare." The Nobel Peace Prize has been awarded to noteworthy individuals who have dedicated their lives for the betterment of mankind. Unfortunately, much of the society has overlooked the individuals who, on a daily basis, wake up each morning with a perception that they may not return home. One may question, "What type of person would subject himself to such unsureness, stress and pressure? What is it inside these individuals that gives them the desire to serve people at the risk of their own personal safety?"

Time after time, surveys taken from children as to what they want to be when they grow up indicates the professions choosen most often are firefighters, police officers, and doctors. It is noteworthy that children at a very early age have the desire to serve their fellow man. The question becomes whether this is a desire that we are born with, or is it the sense of

11

authority and respect that we desire at a young age? Whatever the reason, we find that at some point in our lives we have a sense of responsibility, unselfishness, justice, and even love, for one another.

Heroes: Who are they? Where do they come from? How can we recognize them? Are there really knights in shining armor? There have been books written and movies produced about heroes. At some point, in almost everyone's life, they have dreamed about rescuing someone from a burning house, saving someone drowning in a pool, or some kind of dramatic incident. Ninety-five percent of the population wants to be recognized for some good deed. But who are the true heroes?

Are they the parents who raise their children to have respect for others, with true morals and values? Are they the single parents who tell their children that all things are possible? Are they the parents, who go without so that their children can have? Everyone, in some form or fashion, has displayed some type of heroism, either in providing for their families, or donating time or money for some worthy cause. Is this a true hero?

Sacrifice: There are individuals who have vowed to

sacrifice their lives for the people they serve. These individuals live one-third of their lives away from their family and loved ones. They live together, eat together and socialize together. Morning, day and night, these individuals have to be ready to act in a matter of seconds and place their lives on the line for others. While most people shudder at the thought of what these individuals have to do, these people do not have the luxury of thinking twice about it. They enter places with death staring them straight in their eyes. Yet, these individuals continue not to think about themselves, but of others. Maybe that's why every man, woman, and child loves a Firefighter.

I have been a Firefighter for seven years. The sacrifices, pressures and stress I go through in my profession are all worth it, I love and enjoy what I do. What keeps me motivated is prayer, my family, a positive attitude and the people I serve. Just to see a smile on someone's face after I have saved his or her life is a wonderful feeling.

Firefighters train day in and day out to perfect our trade. Each fire has its own personality and because of this, there is much risk. A typical day for a firefighter starts with the afternoon training at approximately 1:00 p.m. Many times the first alarm dispatches over the intercom during this time. Immediately, everyones' heart begins to race. The fire is in the fifth district this means that crew has to go first. The other crews race to their apparatus. As the engines, squad and tower races down the street, the dispatcher announces over the radio, "receiving repeated calls and smoke showing." At this point, heart rate increases, blood pressure rises and prayers go up.

While racing down the busy streets the district engine crew quickly goes over their plan of action. Suddenly, the smell of smoke is detected. The firefighter turns around in the seat and sees a cloud of smoke far off. The only thing that goes through his mind is that he gets to pull the first hose line of attack. As the district engine pulls up to the fire and sees the flames and smoke coming out of the doors and windows, the officer and firefighter look at each other with a serious smile as they begin to stretch their line.

The officer and firefighter drop to their knees and mask up. The officer then calls out to the driver and tells him he's ready for water. The firefighter opens up the nozzle and knocks down the fire at the door. As he moves closer to the sear of the fire, the temperature rises to 1000 degrees and his adrenaline increases even higher. The glow of the flames is the only source of light. The thick black smoke surrounds them as they enter the apartment. They smother the glowing flames with water and after they are sure that even hidden areas have been sprayed they exit. As they exit the crowd looks upon them and the glow in their eyes are as if they are looking at knights in shinning armor. While the attack crew changes their bottles and takes a drink of water, the rest of the crew enters the apartment to begin the salvage and overhaul.

After everything is over, everyone looks back at the apartment and states, "that was a good stop." The district crew knows that they were the first ones in and will be the last one to leave. But that doesn't bother them because "First ones in and last ones out," is a motto of this profession. Firefighters are a special breed that have been blessed to disregard race, religion, or creed. We truly believe that there is a special place in God's heart for firefighters.

Regardless of which profession you are in, succeeding takes a genuine concern and love for your fellow man. You must earn respect, by giving respect to the people you serve. There are many people who go day after day to a job they feel trapped in with no avenue of escape. Life is too short for anyone not to utilize each and every day to its fullest potential. There should not be a day that goes by that you do not have something positive to say to someone. Your attitude and demeanor play a vital role as to how people perceive you and respond to you.

Possessing a service attitude in your daily work

environment decreases stress and burnout. I have always questioned people as to why they continue to work in an environment that is not conducive to their well being. Perhaps, financial dependency, lack of education, and low self-esteem are some of the reasons. Yet true success comes from a satisfaction that money, education nor any other financial good can bring.

Further, I truly believe that association brings assimilation. If you associate with positive people, not only will you think positive, but you will begin to look at the positive in people rather than the negative. I believe that I have been blessed beyond my wildest dreams. I have been able to associate with people who are like-minded, who possess the same goals and aspirations in life; people who are not looking for any pat on the back or rewards. A firefighters' reward is the pure satisfaction that they were able to help and enrich someone's life. Isn't that what life is all about?

TODAY IS WHAT YOU MAKE IT

L.B. Thigpen
Human Resource

Today is what you make it
Tomorrow you'll never know
Right now is what will matter
Be ready to move and grow

Don't sit there stuck and waiting
For a boost that never comes
For God's promised you something
So get on your feet and run

Rejoice in what He's promised
It's yours and yours alone
Be happy and be grateful
You're never far from home

If home is where your heart is
And if your heart's with Him
You'll never have to worry
There's nothing more to fear

And if you fall or stumble
Begin the begin again
And never should you worry
Just put your faith in Him

For God is the solution
To whatever comes your way
From Him just seek the courage
And never stray away

For those who ask receive it
For those who knock shall find
The door will swing wide open
God's love is so sublime.

DARE TO BE FIRST

A Pioneer is one who does something that no one else has been compelled to do!

DARE TO BE THE FIRST

DAILY REFLECTION

The rewards in life many times come from stepping into unconquered grounds. If you find yourself attracted to fields that are untampered, know that every new ground is broken by someone like you. Meditate on the following:

> For the Father loveth the Son, and
> sheweth him all things that himself doeth:
> and he will shew him greater works
> than these, that ye may marvel.

> John 5:20
> King James Version

The Ladies In Blue

Faye S. Manigault, Bridgette O. Sears
And K. Shawn Urqhuart, Law Enforcement Officers

It takes tremendous courage to be a police officer. And, being a female officer, in a male dominated field, can require additional strength. I started in the field of law enforcement 16 years ago. Because the field is a male dominated profession, I found it particularly challenging. Over the years, I have managed to adjust to the stereotypes through working in various law enforcement agencies. Through this exposure, I realized that women bring a different value and attitude to the field. Realizing this, along with my exposure through the different agencies, gave me the confidence necessary to succeed. I am now in management and supervise over eighty-seven male and female officers.

Of course, because female officers are so rare, we share a common bond. This leads us to share information, resources and leadership skills. As I began to write this book, I spoke with two of my friends who are also in the law enforcement field. The three of us usually get together several times a year to talk about the many different events that have happened during the course of the year. It is truly a blessing to have such good friends who have a strong spiritual foundation and are committed to helping others.

***

It was cold but bright that afternoon when I was called to an accident scene. As I stepped out of the police car to investigate, it was apparent that the small entangled Honda had caused the accident.

The ambulance soon arrived and began to delicately remove the victims out of their cars. As they pulled and gently placed the young girl who was in the Honda on the stretcher, her face caught my attention. I knew her, I looked closer and recognized that the young girl was the daughter of a fellow officer.

At that moment, when I saw her face, my stomach turned and my internal struggle began. What should I do? I had never been faced with giving someone I know a citation, especially when they were so injured. Certainly, to write my coworker's daughter a ticket would appear insensitive.

I slowly put my ticket book back in my pocket as the ambulance drove away. I stared at the wreckage for a few more minutes and then looked down at the ground. This was a serious accident with serious injuries. The wreckers arrived, loaded the cars and drove off.

When I arrived at the police station I immediately talked to the lieutenant. "Take care of it, do what you know is right," he said dismissing me. Well, I knew what I had to do. Later that day I mustered up the courage and drove to my co-workers house. He answered the door and his happiness to see me soon turned to a frown and then to anger as he read the citation. I knew I had done what was right but it sure didn't feel like it.

My internal struggle didn't subdue for two days. Every time I thought about the incident I became sick to my stomach. In a way I felt that I had betrayed a friend, but yet I knew that it wouldn't have been fair to the other driver if I hadn't given my friend's daughter a ticket.

Much to my surprise two days later my friend approached me with a smile. "Thanks for being compassionate and professional throughout this whole ordeal," he said reaching out his hand to shake mine. I grinned ear to ear as I reached my hand out to shake his. Sometimes it takes tremendous courage and strength to do the right thing, especially when people initially disagree.

Bridgette has been in law enforcement for thirteen years.

She has worked in various areas such as campus officer, state trooper, transit officer, and undercover officer with a large municipal task force. She states that her motivating factor and strength are a combination of things such as courage, prayer, meditation, recognition of divine order, faith, and knowing that God is omnipotent. She states, "During my tenure in the field of law enforcement I have been exposed to evil forces that required me to lift up the name of Jesus and use the word of God as a shield and guide. When things appear to be out of control, I affirm that I'm a child of God. So, if God is for me, who can be against me? This affirmation immediately releases me from fear and moves me into feeling safe and protected."

Law enforcement is a unique field, it can evoke every emotion there is from fear to happiness not only in the officers but also in the people we serve. Because of this, I feel that through law enforcement I am being an instrument of God and that is very rewarding. I can lift up people who are oppressed, suppressed, and discouraged about life. Not only am I a channel for them, but their situation reminds me of how blessed I am as well.

Also, being a law enforcement sergeant forces me to discipline other officers at times, this puts me in an awkward position. I maintain my courage and strength by using the

Bible which keeps me fair and impartial. I've found that the Bible is a road map in my life; it guides me through rough periods and reveals stories about righteous servants that went through heavy storms, but at the end were victorious. Two of the most encouraging thoughts to me are that I can hide in the shelter of the Most High, and that God is truly my refuge and fortress. One of my favorite thoughts that I have written to help stay motivated is:

Sleep No More

"For a man that sleeps, sleeps through opportunity.
Dreams and visions are seen through physical sleep
but a man that mentally sleeps misses out on
unexpected opportunities.
Today I will make my dream a reality."

***

Shawn has been a Georgia State Trooper for twelve years. She started as a radio operator. Remarkably, within six months, Shawn was promoted to trooper cadet. At that time there were only two black female troopers in the state of Georgia. Since then, the number has increased to six.

Shawn enjoys her work and supports the mission. She reminisces about the many traffic stops she's made. When the 5'4", 140 lbs female officer steps out of the patrol car, the expression on the violator's face tells it all and on this particular day it was no exception. A car sped past doing 72 in a 55 mile per hour speed zone. Shawn flipped on her blue lights and sped off after the brown Seville. The brown Seville pulled off the road with Shawn right behind it. "Step out of your vehicle," Shawn said as she approached the rear of the Seville.

"What did I do and why are you stopping me," the balding man yelled stepping out of his car. Shawn unemotionally told the man why she had stopped him. He frown and angrily reached in his pocket for his drivers license. Shawn continue to talk with the man in an nice, moderate and even tone. Her tone and mannerism seemed to be releasing the man from his anger. He signed the ticket and then apologized for being so rude.

"Earlier today I was stopped by another state trooper and he was so rude and nasty, I guess when you stopped me I was expecting the same thing," he said thanking Shawn for helping to change his perception of all troopers. On the streets Shawn is called # 827. This number is just another name she has had for ten years.

Shawn states,"Being a female trooper is not easy. It seemed that I had to work much harder to prove myself. It is a known fact that females are not expected to accomplish their mission because of the many challenges and obstacles that exist in this field. Knowing this, I did not let the negative feedback from my fellow male officers inhibit my performance. Instead, I fed off the negative energy and channeled it into a positive drive. Of course, there are good days along with some bad days, but I don't let the bad days take over. I allow the good days to be my shining star. I utilize prayer and meditation to keep me focused and in-line.

What motivates me to stay in this line of work? First of all, the people whom I am able to help. To help someone makes all the difference. Even when I write a person a ticket, they always say thank you. I explain to the violators why I stopped them, and talk to them with respect and love. I've found that communication and courtesy is so important in my line of work. This is what I practice and stress to others officers.

Another motivator is my involvement with several community groups, schools, and youth programs. This allows me to stay focused on the larger picture. I am grateful that God gives me the strength and necessary tools to inspire others.

Finally, in this line of work, I must be strong, have faith and a positive attitude to continue this journey. Each day challenges me to live out my dreams and focus on the reality I wish to create."

***

The memories just go on and on and the stories never end. Being a cop is not easy. One mess up and the media scrutinizes all in BLUE. But not all cops are bad, many are your friends, relatives, and loved ones. They are good, strong, and trustworthy people who must love their jobs in order to stay in this line of work.

Success in this line of work depends on several things. First, one must have the ability to become a team player. No one officer can be successful alone, it takes interdependence. Secondly, it takes a drive to grow, making a commitment and holding yourself accountable. Thirdly, it takes good self-esteem. I always ask myself, "What do I believe about me?" I must love myself, be open-minded, ready and willing to receive whatever comes my way. The real challenge is having great expectations and the will to convert them into positive outcomes.

Finally, as I write this story, I am reminded that all those who wear blue are courageous officers who put their lives on the line to do the right thing. The many sacrifices they must often make to survive are still worth it. I thank every officer in this line of work for taking the many risks that keep others safe. This profession is very challenging, exciting and rewarding as long as there is motivation and devotion to doing the right thing at all times.

The relationship that all officers share as professionals is profound and I am grateful to have the opportunity to share my experience as it relates to this profession. What keeps me motivated after all of these years? Prayer, upward mobility in my professional and personal life, and the opportunity to share the process with others. Keep motivation alive. It is worth it!

THROUGH ME

Yoquieta "Ke Ke" Truitt
Police Officer

Perhaps it sound whimsical. . .

I want to be a doctor, no a lawyer, maybe even a nurse No. . .

I want to be a police officer to work the streets and deal with crime and hate
maybe I'll be a construction worker or engineer, no scratch that I am going to be a scientist.

You know maybe I'll just get married and raise kids. I can be a stay at home mother. That way I can mold my kids to be great. You know God I just want to be what you want me to be. . .

My child you came here with a purpose—I have given you all that you need—I even gave you the right to choice. . .

Just remember, "It's not by might, nor by power, but by my spirit," said the lord of hosts.

You can do or be anything as long as you do it through me.

THE HIDDEN

MEANING

It is less what you are doing; it is more who you
are BEING!

THE HIDDEN MEANING

DAILY REFLECTION

Sometimes it's difficult to know why you are really at a place or experiencing a certain relationship. You may be asking yourself "what purpose am I serving." Rest assured that all things are always in "Divine Order" and the answers that you seek are also seeking you. To help you find the hidden meaning, meditate on the following words:

Trust the Lord with all thine heart;
and lean not unto thine own understanding.
In all thy ways acknowledge him,
and he shall direct thy path.

Proverbs 3:5-6
King James Version

Our unique personality allows human spirit to keep on going to reach a ray of hope. Your health is like rays of light emanating from the sun. Please keep your energy fed.
Do the right thing and say NO to drugs.

CAN YOU READ BETWEEN THE LINES

Walter A. Clark, Jr.
Pharmacist

"Good morning Mr. Mathis. How are you today?" exclaimed the pharmacy clerk, Tony.

"I'm here to pick up my medicine. Is it ready yet?" Mr. Mathis screamed at Tony.

"I'm sure it's ready Mr. Mathis. Let me check on it," Tony said.

"Well hurry up, the senior citizens bus is blowing for me and I'm on my last Depend!" Mr. Mathis was a regular customer at the pharmacy. He always appeared to be angry or upset about something. For some reason we could never seem to please him. It was as though some catastrophe had happened to him and he was mad at the world. Our pharmacy has a lot of senior citizens as customers and many of them show symptoms of despair and loneliness.

I was one of two pharmacists in this retail giant, trying to please our customers and management at the same time. "Well, here's your prescription Mr. Mathis, and the Iron tablets the doctor prescribed are over the counter on aisle four. Here I'll show you," said Tony.

"You mean I waited five-minutes and you still don't have all my medication? I called here earlier and that lady pharmacist told me you had the Iron tablets here," he yelled.

"Mr. Mathis we do have Iron tablets, but they are not prescription items, so we keep them over here on aisle four," Tony tries to explain.

"What's the price and why is it not covered on my Easy Rx insurance card?" Mr. Mathis asked cutting off Tony.

The pharmacist, that's me, comes over to rescue Tony from Mr. Mathis. "I'm sorry Mr. Mathis is there a problem?" I asked.

"You bet your sweet bippy there's a problem; I told that lady pharmacist this morning I needed some Iron tablets and to run my Viagra prescription on my Easy Rx insurance card. Now can you tell me who's in charge of this so called pharmacy?"

"Calm down Mr. Mathis, we don't have a lady pharmacist working here and we never have. You may have talked to one of the female clerks. The prescriptions you need are not covered by your Easy Rx insurance plan. If you want, I can give you a smaller quantity to make it more affordable," I explained.

"All right hurry up and ring me up. I'm late for the bus. I'll never come to this place again, just transfer all of my prescriptions elsewhere!" Mr. Mathis exclaims.

Well, it was another typical day at the local pharmacy beginning with Mr. Mathis. It wouldn't be a normal day if someone didn't run out threatening to transfer to another pharmacy. Is this what I went five years to pharmacy school for? I use to blame myself for choosing a career in pharmacy, but did I really choose pharmacy, or did God choose pharmacy for me? For a long time, I dreaded coming to work. It seemed that my day consisted of angry customers, being short of help, and reporting to greedy management. But, my wife's words inspired me to look at things differently. She said, "You never know who you may be helping."

This made me think, maybe God has a purpose or task for us when we find ourselves in difficult places to work or to live. It may be just a matter of reading between the lines when dealing with difficult people and situations. Maybe we have to ask, why am I really here and why are they, what help are they really seeking, is it love, hope, security or just to know someone cares?

I wonder, do other pharmacists have the same problems? Robbie, the other pharmacy clerk answers the phone and informs me I have a call. It's my supervisor on the line. He gives me a long list of do's and don'ts for the week. He wants me to increase sales 50%, cut staff 60%, fill all the counters with merchandise, give all the doctors in the area discount coupons, stay until 4:00 a.m. for a computer upgrade, fire any employees with overtime, and work the next three holidays. I hung up immediately in order to stay faithful to God's purpose.

The phone rings again for me, this time its Mrs. Hoffler, an elderly lady with Alzheimer disease, that lives in the senior citizens home. "Good afternoon, Mrs. Hoffler, how are you doing today?"

"I'm doing fine. I want to ask you about my medication. Is there any aspirin in my cough medication? You know I can't take aspirin because of my ulcer!" she said.

I knew her history particularly since she calls me everyday to remind me about it. I explained to her there was no aspirin in her medication. She thanked me and hung up. It is a blessing to give out information to people who really want and need it. Mrs. Hoffler called six more times that afternoon with the same question.

Well, it was almost time to close. I was ready to go, I had been working as the only pharmacist for twelve-hours, with no lunch break or bathroom break. My body was trapped between hunger and going to the bathroom. (Most pharmacists don't get lunch or bathroom breaks. It could be risky getting your prescription at the end of the day). As I was saying, it was 8:45 p.m. and we were cleaning up and finishing our last prescriptions, when Ms. Jones came up to the counter with an antibiotic prescription and an insurance card. Ms. Jones was scheduled to have major surgery in the morning and had to have this antibiotic.

When I ran the prescription through the system, I got a rejection that said Easy Rx insurance company did not cover this antibiotic. The medication was too expensive for Ms. Jones. Ms. Jones began to panic because she had to have surgery the following morning. It was now 9:30 p.m. and Ms. Jones would not leave until I did something. My staff was gone, and there was no one to contact at Easy Rx insurance company. I called her doctor five times and got a recording that hung up on me. Also, the prescription that was written for Ms. Jones had an error on the dosage, and Ms. Jones started crying. She needed my help.

My wife and children were expecting me at 9:10 p.m. I told Ms. Jones to calm down. I would give her an estimated dose of the medication and contact her doctor and insurance company in the morning. She was very grateful and left. I wonder sometimes if that's my reason for being here, or is it Mrs. Hoffler, or Mr. Mathis, or someone I haven't yet met? Whatever it is, I'll continue to draw encouragement from my church worship experience, prayer and bible study to find the hidden meaning until God chooses me for another task or assignment.

ETERNAL ELEMENT

Floyd Lee Shannon, Jr.
Poet

Night and day every minute covered by the hands of good intentions.

Needs and wants hang in the balance.

To do what must be done, the true mother of all invention.

Untold obstacles placed in the path, self-doubt rear its ugly head.

To continue is to the test; to give up is the fear.

Who keeps the score? The life game is continual, everlasting.

First dawn breaks. Is this the beginning or the end?

Night bares the same black and blue bruises. Ah! same difference.

To carry on in the face of adversity, it's an uphill battle.

Tears flow, the cup runs over, the baked earth cares not from where the moisture came.

From devastation comes hope, out of the ashes seeds of faith spring forth.

The battle of want versus need versus means wages on.

The soldiers of compassion are marching.

The torch of humanity sometimes flickers; the flame burns oh so low.

From the front to the back, the view of the needy looks the same.

A helping hand, a kind word, which uttered the phrase live and let live?

Through the fog a light shines, a bay of hope, a hesitant wish.

For whom the bell tolls, upward, skyward to the clouds.

To the forefront rushes the blessed individual, one soul, one spirit believing he can make a difference.

THE MIRACLE

IN THE VALLEY

Even in moments of great turmoil there is a gift
in it for YOU!

THE MIRACLE IN THE VALLEY

DAILY REFLECTION

Many times God gives us something to move us truly into our divine space.

In moments of despair or tragedy there are great lessons and growth opportunities. If you find yourself in a space of despair or tragedy know that there is a miracle in it for you. Meditate on the following words:

For all things are for your sakes, that the abundant
grace might through the thanksgiving
of many rebound to the glory of God.

II Corinthians 4:15
King James Version

42

Every effort you make is a process of learning, improving and developing self-skills to increase productivity and service. Believing in yourself and having self-initiative helps you develop the faith to rise above any adversity.

A Learning Process

Mae L. Johnson
Retired Teacher

I teach! Teaching was not my first love, nor my first choice for a lifelong profession, although my elementary and secondary school years were positive experiences for me. I loved going to school and was an avid reader and learner. Whenever I thought of what I would like to be, it was always something I thought exciting; like a nurse, a musician, a world traveler, maybe a wife and a mother. Teaching was never in the forefront.

A series of flukes led me to teaching. At the beginning, I was instilled with a love for learning by my aunt and uncle who raised me. They were teachers, and they were good ones who loved what they did for the poor migrant children with poor uneducated migrant parents. Living with my Aunt and Uncle exposed me to reading all kinds of educational materials, wonderful conversations with their friends, and traveling all over the state with them. It was a foregone conclusion in their minds that I would become a teacher, but my adolescent rebellion said that I would NOT become a teacher, but maybe a nurse, or maybe a musician, or maybe a travel agent. (I didn't know any travel agents, but it sounded good, anyway). But, succumbed by my aunt and uncle wishes, I went off to college and majored in elementary education and minored in library science. And, when I graduated from college, I was handed a teaching job.

I found out two things about teaching: TEACHING IS HARD WORK! What you learn in college (theory) is entirely different from what it is like in the classroom (practice). THERE IS NOT MUCH $$$ BEING PAID TO TEACHERS. After twenty-two years of every need being supplied by my guardians, it was difficult to live on a teacher's salary. So I left the teaching profession for the only other thing that my undergraduate school prepared me for, I became an army librarian. Maybe that would prepare me for being a travel agent, I thought.

A librarian has access to so much material, so many books, and comes in contact with so many people. That is an education within itself. Along the way, I met a man that I married and had his children. We traveled all over the United States as well as the Far East. I was happy!

If this piece were a movie, the music would change from being light and springlike to heavy organ bass. It would alert you to the fact that something was going to happen to this idyllic time in my life. Something did happen. Our son was diagnosed as learning disabled.

Okay. I could fix it. After all, I was a teacher. I could teach him to speak and to read, couldn't I? WRONG!!! Nothing in my life or my schooling had prepared me for this. Specific Learning Disorders is a whole new ball game in the field of education. So, I went back to college full-time to get a graduate degree in Special Education.

To me learning was still fun, and I already knew the difference between theory and practice. Somewhere in my mind was that after I had fixed my son's disability, I would go back into the classroom and fix some other students' disabilities, too. OK, I was psyched. I was going to turn this Special Education thing around. Little did I know that this Special Education thing turned my life around.

I received my Masters of Education degree, and went back into the classroom. Only this time, I had a plan, and everything was going to be different. Right! I immediately learned two things. TEACHING IS HARD!!! and TEACHING LEARNING DISABLED AND LOW ACHIEVING

45

STUDENTS IS EVEN HARDER! Trying to sell your program to "regular" education colleagues, learning tolerance, and trying to teach academics while attending to the needs of the students are but a few of the many functions in this diverse world of teaching.

That's the hard part but what are the rewards? I was told, and truly believed that "teaching is a noble and rewarding profession." Noble? Rewarding???

Special students are needy:

they need attention

they need access to information at their levels

they need goals

they need intervention

they have little experience; hence, little on which to build a foundation.

As an African-American teacher, I found that African-American students subjected me to much more scrutiny. I had to develop a real sense of humor, to gain respect from them. First, I thought their questions invaded my privacy:

Are you a "real" teacher?

Do you have any children?

Do you have a husband?

Does he live in the house with you and your

children?

Does he work?

Does he help pay the rent and buy the groceries?

Then I found the students just as eager to share their lives with me as wanting to know all about my life. I now consider myself lucky to be able to teach, to be able to work with those who really need what I can offer. The reward has not been monetary, but the awareness that I have made a difference in someone's life.

After 12 years in the teaching profession, I am now preparing to retire. Yet, my concerns continue to be the students. I ask:

Who is going to reassure these children that they have value?

Who will give them the attention they crave?

Who will clarify the assignments they do not quite understand?

Who will congratulate and compliment them when they have successfully accomplished a goal?

Who will admonish, correct or discipline them when they need to be admonished, corrected or disciplined?

Who will admire their work, their style, and their strengths?

Who will provide them with a safe environment in which

they can learn?

Who will laugh with them, comfort them?

Who will LOVE them?

WHO WILL TEACH THEM?

So, while I reflect on the calm and peace of my forthcoming retirement, these questions haunt me. I realize that I can't totally retire from this profession that I have come to truly love. I realize that my calling is to be a teacher today, tomorrow and always. I'm devoted to teaching and to the children whom I have yet met. To satisfy this devotion and concern I will teach on a substitute basis until I can't teach any more!

PAGE OF LIFE

Floyd Lee Shannon Jr.
Poet

I've walked the road of circumstance.
I've ridden the highway of self-doubt.
It was only through Christ my savior, that I truly learned
what life was all about.

See I awoke as if from a haze.
Obstacles used to be my guide.
Into the shadows of the unknown he spread his light.
Now his guidance and his strength fill my weary soul with
pride.

I no longer fear nor dread the unknown.
The unbelievers may do, as they will.
I've learned each day to praise my Lord Jesus.
See that lifts me higher than any doctor's pill.

Some have laughed and called me ugly names.
For them I pray, I truly hope enough.
I have only to think of God's servant Job.
Then life's bumpy roads hardly seem so rough.

This course of action that I've taken, I know, is not for
everyone.
To the deep inner self one must be true.
The course chose me, I didn't choose it.
I must do what I must do.

CLAIMING

YOUR OWN

Every business there is, began with someone like
you, someone with strong desire and intent!

CLAIMING YOUR OWN

DAILY REFLECTION

You are the captain of your own ship. This means you have a choice on what kind of life you wish to create. Being your own boss is an option available to you. Yes, it takes a great deal of courage and faith to step out there on your own. But if it is something you truly desire, success can certainly be yours.

If you are pondering the possibility of beginning your own business, then meditate on the following words:

This book of the law shall not depart out of thy mouth; but shall meditate therein day and night, that thou mayest observe to do according to all that is written therein: for then thou shalt make thy way prosperous, and then thou shalt have good success. Have not I commanded thee? Be strong and of a good courage; be not afraid, neither be thou dismayed: for the lord thy God is with the whithersoever thou goest.

Joshua 1:8-9
King James Version
52

You can do whatever your heart desires
You control your destiny
You set the standards for yourself
You are the boss
Stay focused, alert, and steadfast and with all of this,
Growth will come at a greater speed.

AN

ENTREPRENEUR'S DREAM

Anthony and Thelma Wright
Entrepreneurs

I 've owned Sir Clean Building Service Inc. since 1984. It's a janitorial service located in Ft. Lauderdale, Florida. During this period it has grown from 4 employees to over 130 employees. Being an entrepreneur is an achievement of a life long dream.

Since childhood, my desire has been to own my own business. Because of this desire, I took my academics very seriously. I wanted to be prepared when the time came to pursue entrepreneurship. I didn't really know what type of business I would own but I knew, deep within, that I would and I never let the dream die.

I majored in Business Administration at Florida A&M

University. College definitely prepared me for a business career. After college I did extensive business research. I started by reviewing the business opportunity section of the local newspaper. Then, I subscribed to a magazine titled *Business Opportunities*. Next, I ordered several business start-up manuals. I also joined an investment group. All of these things exposed me to many opportunities. Ultimately, I chose to pursue the janitorial business, it was something I had done before and was somewhat familiar with.

One day back in 1983, I found a janitorial firm in the local newspaper for sale. I contacted the owners and told them I was interested in buying their business. My research had taught me to accumulate as much knowledge as possible about any business investment, so I asked the owners if I could work for them for a while. They agreed and I worked for them for two months without pay. After the second month I decided to move forward with the purchase. By March of 1984, the purchase transaction was completed, and I began the transformation of Sir Clean into the business it is today.

The first year of being in business was the most challenging, but yet exciting and satisfying. On top of starting a new business, Themla and I were expecting our first child. I knew from all the articles that I had read, I could very well be forced to maintain a second job in addition to running my business. Sure enough, this was the case. I knew I had financial responsibilities towards my business and an obligation to support my family. I kept my full-time job at the telephone company for an entire year.

Yet, sooner or later an entrepreneur must make the decision to "break out." I did this when I felt that my entrepreneur spirit would not jeopardize the well being of Thelma and our child. I did not want them to have to sacrifice or want because of my desire to claim my own dream. If sacrifices were to be made, it would be on my end. My strength to work two full time jobs came from the love of Thelma and our daughter.

One may ask, "what does it take to stay in business?" I would say it takes three things not only to stay in business but also to consider before going into business in the first place. They are DESIRE, COMMITMENT, and SACRIFICES. Being an entrepreneur can be very difficult and quite challenging. Therefore, you must really want to accept this challenge and be willing to commit the time, energy, and resources to make it work. I've seen people accomplish a lot of things: some small and others large, but despite the size you can rest assured it took wanting something strongly enough (the DESIRE) and doing whatever it takes (the COMMITMENT) and the patience to allow it to happen (the SACRIFICES) to be successful.

The first year of business is the time for learning. I don't think there is any work experience that can fully prepare you for entrepreneurship. As an entrepreneur you must become proficient in marketing, sales, operations, bookkeeping, and personnel just for beginners. There are all types of challenges you face every day. Most businesses prepare a business plan prior to starting, but it's actually in the first year of business that your business plan evolves. The first year in business is when you really begin to understand how, when, and where you need to market your product and/or service, and who your customers will be. The best way to approach the first year is to keep an open mind, pray, and understand that you must go through a learning phase, and you don't have all the answers.

As an entrepreneur, I thrive on the feeling of independence and the control I have over my personal life. That's a big part of what motivates me and allows me to stay in business. I am also motivated by the new challenges I face, sometimes daily. Entrepreneurship is tough and grueling but the personal reward of success fuels a burning desire to achieve more.

Having my family involved with the business has also been rewarding. My wife, Thelma, has been part owner of our business since the beginning; however, in the beginning we did not have the same motivation. As I mentioned earlier, owning my own business was a life long dream for me but it wasn't for Thelma. Our relationship allowed me the flexibility to do whatever was necessary to build the business, and as the business grew my dream became Thelma's dream and now we both work for our company.

The first advice I would give anyone who is interested in entrepreneurship is that it isn't for everyone. Then, I would ask if you really had the DESIRE to do this. Note I said, "Do this," not "Try this." Tryers seldom succeed, only doers are successful. Next I would ask are you COMMITTED to doing whatever it takes and are you willing to make the SACRIFICES it takes to achieve success. If you've answered yes to all of these, I would say the battle is half won because entrepreneurship is a journey that never has to end. It's a journey that's bound only by your imagination. If you have determined that entrepreneurship is for you, now is the time to begin your research to determine what it is you want to do.

Once you feel the thrill of success as an entrepreneur, it is very difficult to return to the workforce. You begin to look at life from a much broader view than most single-function job assignments and therefore having a job doesn't seem challenging enough.

Entrepreneurship is the most challenging and rewarding ventures you could ever do for yourself. Oh bye the way, we have started our second business venture, a retail salvage store named price cutters.

LIVE UP TO YOUR POTENTIAL

James Tripp Mitchell
Investigator

A fundamental responsibility in this world is to live up to your own potential. Each individual has something different they want to achieve and have a different force driving them to it. No two people have the same amount of potential. By living up to your potential, you can assure yourself of the highest standard of excellence and reward yourself with success. We all have goals and dreams.

Motivation is the driving force within that allows us to achieve those goals and dreams. That's why I believe motivation is directly related to potential. You have to be willing to cut through life's red tape and stand in that never-ending line that winds endlessly. Motivation is a mind set, not a feeling. Even if you love your job, family and life there is still room for improvement. You may have to focus in on your priorities, but once you have, it becomes easier to achieve success.

My simple equation is
motivation + potential = success.

FIGHTING THE BATTLE

There are times in each of our lives when we feel we must fight, wearing the armour of God allows us to fight with equity!

FIGHTING THE BATTLE

DAILY REFLECTION

Being called to fight can be devastated. Just the idea of a battle brings fear, confusion and frustration to most people minds. Yet, most change has occurred through a battle rather mental or physical. When you are called to fight a battle consider God's purpose. Consider the change that might occur upon a victory.

If you are in the midst of a battle with yourself or others, meditate on the following:

Put on the whole armour of god,
that ye may be able to stand against the wiles of the devil.
For we wrestle not against flesh and blood, but against
principalities, against powers, against the rulers of the
darkness of this world,
against spiritual wickedness in high *places.*

Ephesians 6:11-12
King James Version
62

Marching On
Do what you must and strive for the sky
The sky is the limit and the choices are yours
You are the only person that can set your goals
Make them attainable so that you can accomplish them
Continue your March and success will prevail

March On, March On to Victory!

MARCHING ON

Demetrius Alphonso Swilley, Sr.
Retired Military Officer

As I prepared to graduate from high school, I looked around and saw many black men having a hard time supporting their children. There didn't seem to be any jobs available and college assistance seemed to be at a minimum. I didn't want to be another statistic so I chose to go to the Army. The Army paid my way to take care of my family and to finish my education.

I entered the army not really knowing what to expect. The first three years I focused on learning the rules and ropes of the military. By the fourth year, I had the opportunity to supervise, teach, train and discipline soldiers. Supervision responsibilities helped me grow in several ways. First of all, it helped me over-come the fear of not being accepted. I had to trust myself and the choices I made. I was now responsible for other people careers. I had to accept the successes and failures of my section and unit and correct any shortcomings.

During this time, I also learned to delegate. Being a hands on manager this was a difficult task but eventually I learned to stand back and not take on all tasks myself. Sharing responsibilities and tasks helped me and others. In others it built confidence and leadership skills so that they could be successful in my absence.

My next tour gave me more responsibilities and the chance to develop more of myself. I believe the tour also made me more competitive for promotions and other jobs. I continued to motivate myself by self-development and realizing my personal worth. This tour also brought me to what we in the service call the "halfway point:" This was the point where I could stay in the service or get out. I sat down with my wife and we decided the best thing for us as a family was for me to stay in for twenty years, get the kids through college and prepare for life on the outside.

My next assignment took me to Korea. Without family, this assignment taught me the meaning of family and how important they are to my well-being. This assignment gave me the opportunity to study and prepare myself for the next level in leadership. I left this assignment and went on to my advanced course that prepared me for one of the most trying times of my life...WAR.

The idea of war left me numb. This is why I was in the army, but the idea of having to kill others and the possibility of being killed myself made me pause and look closely at my life. When my unit moved from Duran to the desert, only 100 miles from Kuwait, I knew it was time. The laughter among the troops ended and everyone became quite serious. It was as if we all grew up overnight.

The fear that emanated through my body each time I saw bomb flash waves in the air is without description. The alarm would sound and I wondered if a scud missile would hit and if so would there be some unknown chemical accompanying it?

The nights were the worst. It was quiet, actually silent, I couldn't even hear a radio. The radio was our only way of knowing what was going on. My heart skipped beats, as the darkness brought me closer to God. I prayed more during this period then I had ever prayed in my life. I prayed for my future, I planned for my future and I prayed for my family. War has a way of making you appreciate and understand the importance of life and what you need to do.

The war ended and I was sent back home to my family.

What a reunion! They seemed to have been just a scared as I was. The reality of the war set in after we returned to the U.S. some soldiers were sick and infected with unknown diseases. If you had not prepared yourself for advancement or was in a Military Occupational Speciality (MOS) that was not in demand, your services were no longer needed, you were forced to retire.

Fortunately, I had prepared for advancement. I had taken advanced courses, cross training, earned a college degree and was in a MOS in demand. Therefore, I was given another assignment.

Fort Bragg, North Carolina became my next home and with it came more pride in my unit. I learned the meaning of the "pucker" factor. This is one of the many sayings you learn in the Army. It is when you allow yourself or others to place pressure on you so bad that you cannot handle things and you lockup and do not perform your tasks or duties. I personally didn't experience this but many of those around me did. It became apparent that Fort Bragg is not for every soldier, and if one has any doubts about the Army, this place will either confirm or dispel them. One will learn to either adapt or have a hard time being there.

At Fort Bragg I was given the opportunity to be in charge

of a lot of people and to guide, train and prepare them for war. One thing I noticed about war is once you have been called upon to do the things you were trained to do and you survive; life becomes very important and you are better prepared mentally for life's success or failure.

What new adventures will I go through before I can say I can stop marching? As many of you know, there is the right time for everything, and everything happens for a reason at the right time. All life's experiences and adjustments require an understanding from one's self. Self-understanding allowed me to become satisfied with my life and gain respect from others. Support from my family meant a lot. Knowing that my family was praying and providing unconditional love allowed me to continue my growth professionally and personally. No matter what assignments or tasks I had to handle, rest assured I could complete all of them with this great support.

So, many ask what really kept me motivated throughout those years? My answer is always the same, "without my family I could never be all I could be." It doesn't matter what the circumstances, my family and their prayer will be there for me when no one else will. I know prayer changes things. Doing 20 was a mind set, I coped, adjusted, changed and accepted the things around me, and now that it's over I'm better off for it.

The service gave me finances and the education to take care of my family, the discipline to handle negativity and the confidence to take on adversity.

After twenty-one years, I now can relax, enjoy my extended family and my home. It has been one year since my retirement and I thank God that I am alive, well and still marching on.

NEVER GET TIRED

Tom E. McBeth
Trainer, Consultant and Author

Prepare your mind during tribulations to keep you from exploding

Acknowledge the power of God in your life and things will begin unfolding

Talk to God about your trials, don't run to friends you know

Imagine the best will only come when you stop and let go

Expect miracles everyday; beyond what your eye can see

Nourish your mind with the word of God and never give into defeat

Claim your victory, shout it out, before you see things manifest

Examine your heart and do your part to be patient until *God bless.*

THE POWER IN

CHANGE

Without change we would never go anywhere; we
would never grow!

THE POWER IN CHANGE

DAILY REFLECTION

Change is crucial to our own development, without it we become stagnated and fall short of fulfilling even a small portion of our potential. There is much power in change, especially when we affirm that every change is for our highest and greatest good.

Take a quick peek at your own life. In what areas can you pinpoint stagnation? In what ways could you definitely expand and then meditate on the following words:

Behold, I tell you a mystery: We shall not all sleep, but we shall all be changed-in a moment, in the twinkling of an eye, at the last trumpet. For the trumpet will sound, and the dead will be raised incorruptible, and we shall be changed.

1 Corinthians 15:51-52
King James Version

The greater the glory, the task will be done.
Quest of knowledge will ensure the path of excellence and prosperity will come forth.

Challenging and Rewarding
Barbara A. Price
Master Hairstylist/Master Barber
Optimum Hair Designs

I guess you could say I have the ultimate twenty-four hours job. I am a business owner, minister's wife and proud mother of two rambunctious school aged sons and daughter who is a toddler. All these aspects of my life have their own unique requirements that contribute to a very full and rewarding life.

Looking back in retrospect, I have always desired to create, design and style hair. After finishing Southeast High School in 1979, my mother encouraged me to attain a Cosmetology Certificate from the community technical school in Bradenton, Florida. However, at the time I had other plans. My plans were to attend Clark Atlanta University where I attained my degree in Business Administration with a concentration in Accounting. While attending college I found my greatest inspiration and motivator for my life was Jesus Christ. On March 21, 1983, I accepted Jesus Christ as my personal Savior. This experience changed my life completely. From as far back

73

as I can remember I desired to have a good life, with a good husband and most of all children.

That experience in 1983 gave me what I needed and saved me at the same time. For seven years, from age fourteen to twenty one, I was living on what many would term the wild side--drugs, parties, premartial sex, and many other daring things. I lived this life but at the same time I often pondered and desired more. Actually my life was miserable. It was a lie and full of confusion. "It must be more to life," I said on my eighteenth birthday. This question followed with, "What am I doing?"

Somehow, even at that time I knew I needed the Lord. As I look back, I recognize that the Lord sent messenger after messenger to tell me about Him. However, although I needed the Lord to take control of my life, I also knew that I wasn't ready. I had a boyfriend and I knew I couldn't be sexually active and unmarried. I knew that once I gave my life over to the Lord that I was going all the way.

At age twenty-one, I had a hard core decision to make. I was pregnant and I had to decide whether to have an abortion or not. I deeply felt it was wrong. I felt it was a lot like premediated murder. However, I couldn't see any other options but to terminate my baby's life. Although the counselor at the clinic constantly said, I was making the right decision. I came to find out later that this wasn't the right decision for me. I was miserable and depressed for weeks. At this point I knew I had to give my life to Chirst. There was no way I could live with such guilt, shame and condemnation. That day I repented and surrendered. Thanks to the Lord, I was able to graduate from college and begin my career as an accountant.

After graduating in 1983, He began to unfold mysteries, gifts, and talents to fulfill my life. I worked several jobs in the corporate arena and constantly found myself unsatisfied. In that realm of "dog-eat-dog" world I decided that if I was going to work hard and long hours it was going to be for me from now on.

In November 1986, I discovered I had the gift to create beautiful floral arrangements, my first customer was myself. I did my first wedding on March 28, 1987. The flowers were so beautiful; I began to get requests to do weddings, banquets, baby showers, bridal showers, and parties. I continued to do the floral business on the side while working in the corporate arena as an accountant. Doing my floral arrangements on the side gave me my first pleasure of being my own boss. I was doing something that I truly enjoyed and the compliments from my customers motivated me to do more.

I found myself more and more disinterested in the politics and deceitfulness it took to move up the corporate ladder of success. Although the success of my floral consultant business made up for the unhappiness I experienced in the corporate arena. One afternoon after being written up for nit picky and petty accusations, I decided enough was enough. It was time to put faith to my commitment. That same afternoon I spoke with the Department Chairperson of Cosmetology, of Atlanta Area Technical School. She really encouraged me to pursue becoming a cosmetologist despite all the odds of working a full-time job, being the mother of two children and at that time pregnant with my third child, a wife and co-laborer with my husband in the ministry.

That day I made a commitment to myself and with the strength of the Lord I knew I could do it. I had a made up mind, and when you have a made up mind to be successful nothing can stop you from being an achiever. You see getting a college education trains you to go get a job and work for someone else. Going to a technical school trains you to become an entrepreneur. My mind had to be reprogrammed to know that I was in bondage and inhibited working for someone else.

I started Atlanta Area Technical School on March 26, 1996, and finished Cosmetology on September 27, 1997, inclusive of the birth of my daughter. I continued in the crossover program for the Barbering Program, which was three months and completed on December 12, 1997. I received my license for Cosmetology December 31, 1997 and my Barbering License on July 13, 1998.

Before completion of school, I looked at several salons from the north side of town to the south and I decided that I could not see starting my career in the red every month paying high booth rentals. I prayed and talked to my husband about my options, and we decided that I had space in my home that was not being utilized, my garage. I began to clean it out and found two gallons of beautiful paint. I painted, and now the only thing I needed was equipment.

On my way home one day after school, I said Lord I need a shampoo bowl. Instantly, my girlfriend came to mind. She had a sister-in-law who had purchased some equipment she wasn't using. I called my girlfriend and she told me that her sister-in-law was the manager of a salon in the mall and they were in the process of renovating. I called her sister-in-law and I was able to buy a shampoo bowl and chair, two hairdryers and two styling chairs, at a price that only God could ordain.

I have been in business now for about one year. It has been quite a challenge in building a clientele, but I am not going to give up. I give out business cards in the grocery lines, at the gas station, wherever. I believe that everybody is a potential client and I am confident in what I do because I am one of the best because of whom my Father is, Jesus Christ.

To some people I am considered a "superwoman" with all the "jobs" I have. However, I don't consider myself a superwoman. I'm just a woman who has been truly blessed with a talent, a husband that I adore and three beautiful children that completes me. I know that these are gifts from my Father Jesus Christ.

CONCLUSION

Glorious Reflections of Strength is a dream I've had for quite some time. The dream is that it will provide motivation twenty-four hours a day. I've found that people are interested in having resource tools for self-knowledge, self-analysis and self-motivation. Therefore, I strongly recommend that you keep a copy of this book close to you. This book is designed to aid in increasing awareness, stimulating a positive attitude, and generating a healthy self-esteem.

The motivators you've met in this book work in a wide variety of fields and have many different backgrounds. Each one of them is an intelligent, enthusiastic, and an energetic person who has provided all of his or her inner secrets in order to make his or her dreams a reality. Hopefully, this book has stressed and delivered the message that motivation is the key to positive doers and positive thinkers, as well as repeating your image endlessly, building stable functioning and increasing awareness of all potential. All people, no matter what their background, must maintain twenty-four hours of motivation to turn around careers and lives.

A special thanks to my best friend, husband, son, and associates whose support allows me to have a pleasant day. The admiration, motivation, and appreciation inspire me to have a good attitude. These roles play a very important part in my daily life.

Feeling good about myself and having a positive attitude motivates me to treat others with dignity and respect. My best friend influences me to face all challenges with a smile each day. Thanks friend; and by the way I would like to share Him with you. He is "Jesus Christ" my motivator.

"MOTIVATION IS CRITICAL FOR ALL"

Contributors

Walter Clark Jr., Atlanta, Georgia
Can You Read Between the Lines

Mae L. Johnson, Raleigh, North Carolina
A Learning Process

Sharma D. Lewis, Atlanta, Georgia
A Life Changing Transformation

Tom E. Mc Beth, Atlanta, Georgia
Never Get Tired

James T. Mitchell (Tripp), Atlanta, Georgia
Living up to Your Potential

Barbara A. Price, Jonesboro, Georgia
Challenging and Rewarding

Bridgette O. Sears, Morrow, Georgia
The Ladies in Blue
Today I Will Work Toward My Purpose

Floyd Shannon, Bradenton, Florida
Page of Life and Eternal Element Poems

Phillip E. Smith, Yispanti, Michigan
True Humanitarians

Demetrius AL. Swilley Sr., Bradenton, Florida
Marching On

L.B. Thigpen, Atlanta, Georiga
Today is What You Make It

Yoquietta "Ke Ke" Truitt, Atlanta, Georgia
Through Me

Carlora Turnquest, Brooklyn, New York
Foreword

Karen Shawn Urqhart, Albany, Georgia
The Ladies in Blue

Anthony and Thelma Wright, Fort Lauderdale, Florida
An Entrepreneur Dream

Resource Centers

The organizations mentioned on this page contains Spiritual, Educational, Uplifting and Motivational Programs that would be a great asset to you and others. I encourage you to make contact.

Job Coalition Network Associations, Inc.
584 Paul Street
Riverdale, Georgia 30274
770-478-5911 or 770-603-6309

McBeth and Associates, Inc.
584 Paul Street
Riverdale, Georgia 30274
770-478-5911 or 770-603-6309
E-mail tem@aol.com

Med-Talk, Inc.
Disease Management
7139 Hwy 85 #153
Riverdale, Georgia 30296
1-800-517-00070
www.med-talk.com

The Merging Worlds Corporations
P.O. Box 2137
Smyrna, Georgia 30081-0998
404-892-8202 or 404-8929757
www.spritualyp.com
E-mail mergingworlds@mindspring.com

Metro Technology Service
P.O. Box 741452
Riverdale, Georgia 30274
770-996-1199 or 770-909-3323
www.Fmanigault@aol.com

TMI Resources, Inc.
P.O. Box 90127
East Point, Georgia 30364-0127
E-mail J T MITCH 3@aol.com

About the Author

Faye Swilley Manigault earned her BS in Criminal Justice at Florida A&M University and her MS in Public and Urban Affairs at Georgia State University. She is a Director of Security at an urban hospital in Atlanta, Georgia. Co-owner of Metro Technology Services and Co-founder of McBeth and Associates, Inc. She Facilitates workshops, seminars and training programs in the areas of Career Development and Safety Issues. Faye is also a youth Motivational Speaker, the contributing author of **Hit the Clock...Workers Words of Wisdom** and the Author of an upcoming book, **Uno is enough, Let's Cope and Stay Motivated**. Faye lives in Atlanta, with her husband, John and son, Jontay. Her personal and professional motto is "Motivation is critical for all".

Order Form

To order additional autographed copies of *Glorious Reflections of Strength* please submit your request with payment to:

**Metro Technology Service
P.O. Box 741452
Riverdale, Georgia 30274
e-mail Fmanigualt@aol.com**

Name: _____

Address: _____

City: _____**State:** _____**Zip:**

_____

I would like to order *Glorious Reflections of Strength*:

_____**Copies @ $10.95 per copy:**   _____

7% GA State Sales Tax ($1.05 ea.)   _____

Shipping & handling ($3.00 ea.)   _____

Total: _____

**Make Checks or Money Orders Payable to
Metro Technology Service.**

*Please allow two to four weeks for delivery.
(Please make copies of this form)*